GW01607278

Victoria Plum

Victoria has a Visitor

Angela Rippon

Illustrated by Frank Wells

Purnell

ISBN 0 361 05582 X

Published 1983 by Purnell Books, Paulton, Bristol, BS18 5LQ
a member of the BPCC group of companies.
Made and printed in Great Britain by Purnell and Sons (Book Production) Limited, Paulton, Bristol

Victoria's Cousin, Sugar Plum

Victoria Plum was sitting outside her front door, reading a book. She could feel the warmth of the sun on her face, and all around her the Great Wood was full of the sounds of summer. The bees were buzzing lazily from flower to flower. The birds were singing a joyful song from the topmost branches of the trees. And the butterflies were dressed in the most beautiful colours.

Victoria sighed. 'This is lovely, what a pity I can't share it with my friends in the Fairy Kingdom.'

Just then Victoria saw a flash of blue through the trees, and the next minute a swallow had landed on the ground in front of her. The long blue feathers of his tail swept the ground, and his snowy white breast heaved up and down as he tried to catch his breath. In his beak he carried a letter. He gave it to Victoria and said breathlessly, "Message from the Fairy Kingdom. Your cousin, Sugar Plum, has finished at the Fairy School, and is coming to stay with you for a while." He took a deep breath, then added hurriedly, "It's all in the letter—must fly," and with that he flashed back through the

trees up into the clear blue sky on the way back to the Fairy Kingdom.

Victoria quickly opened the letter and read: "Dear Cousin Victoria, Now that I have finished at Fairy School I have become a woodland fairy and must find a home of my own in the Great Wood. While I am looking for a little house, please may I come and stay with you? I shall be arriving on Sunday. Love, Sugar."

Victoria was delighted. But then she suddenly thought, 'Coming on Sunday. My goodness, that's tomorrow!' And she rushed back into the house to get

the spare bedroom ready. She dusted and polished all the furniture. She put clean sheets on the bed, and was just putting a vase of fresh woodland flowers in the room, when her friend Benjamin the Elf, burst into the house full of excitement. "I've just had some marvellous news," he said. "One of my old friends called Eric is coming to stay for a few weeks, and he's arriving tomorrow."

Then Victoria told Ben that *she* was having a visitor too, and suggested that they all come round to her house for tea on Sunday afternoon. Ben thought that was a marvellous idea. "We can all be friends together then," he said excitedly.

The next day Victoria made biscuits and scones and a

special plum cake for tea. Just when everything was ready there was a knock at the door. Victoria opened it—and there was Sugar Plum. She was dressed in a frothy white dress tied with a large pink sash around the waist. On her feet she wore tiny pink shoes, and on her head a large floppy white hat. She was so tiny that Victoria felt quite tall. It was ages since Victoria had seen Sugar, but she had always been fond of her tiny cousin, and was delighted that she'd come to stay. Victoria gave Sugar a hug, showed her to her room, and then helped her to unpack. All of her clothes were pink and white and very dainty. Victoria decided that Sugar was just like her name, sweet little thing, and she knew it wouldn't be long before everyone in the Great Wood would come to know her and love her.

While the two fairies got everything ready for tea,

they talked about their friends and family. Sugar gave Victoria all the news from the Fairy Kingdom, and Victoria told Sugar about the Great Wood. At 4 o'clock precisely the door burst open and there was Ben with his friend Eric the Elf. Eric didn't wait to be introduced, or invited in. He barged through the room, sat in Victoria's favourite chair and started tucking into the food.

All through tea he talked about himself. How good he'd been at school. How he'd won all the Elf flying races. How he was best at this and top at that. He didn't want to hear about anyone else, and when Sugar timidly began to say that she'd just left school and was going to look for a house in the Great Wood, Eric butted in loudly, saying that she would be much better off looking for somewhere in the Green Wood, where he lived. "It's much nicer than here," he said.

Victoria was very upset. She loved the Great Wood, but Eric didn't seem to care how rude he was, or what he said. So when tea was over, Victoria was very grateful that Ben and Eric went home. She had been friends with Ben for ages, and didn't want to hurt his feelings. But privately she decided that she didn't like Eric at all and hoped that she wouldn't see much of him during his two week's holiday.

The next morning Victoria took Sugar Plum for a walk through the Great Wood. They met the snails and the robins, spiders and field mice. Everyone was charmed by Victoria's dainty little cousin. They were also amused by the way she always flew lightly over muddy patches and puddles instead of sloshing through them like everyone else.

Sugar said, "I don't like getting my shoes dirty," and

Victoria just laughed. "I enjoy walking through the puddles," she said, "so if you ever change your mind, Sugar, I'll be only too happy to lend you a pair of wellington boots."

But Sugar just wrinkled up her nose. "I really don't like dirt," she said sweetly, and lightly flew off to a dry patch on the path.

Eric Is Very Naughty

The two fairy friends had a wonderful morning. There were so many creatures to visit and places to see. They had a salad lunch with the rabbits, and a tea of nuts and berries with the blackbirds. But at last it was time to start making their way home.

When they were not far from Victoria's house they heard a small creature whimpering. In the long grass beside the path Victoria found a small field mouse. His long tail, which was usually so slim and straight, was tied in a jumble of the most complicated knots.

"How on earth did you manage that?" Victoria asked kindly.

But the mouse just wouldn't stop crying. "It was that horrible Elf," he sobbed. "I was just sitting here minding my own business when he came along and tied my tail in knots. Oh, I'll never get them out! It's such a horrible mess."

Victoria told him not to worry. "I can straighten that out in no time," she said. And with a quick wave of her hand and a scattering of fairy dust, the knots were undone, and the mouse had a lovely, long straight tail again. Victoria hoped that the episode was nothing more than a silly prank, and when she and Sugar got home they forgot all about it.

But the very next day the two fairies came across a group of small hedgehogs running around in circles and crying loudly. "Whatever's the matter?" said Victoria.

The eldest hedgehog boy pointed up to the branches of a tall tree and said, "It's our baby brother, he's trapped up there and we just don't know how to get him down."

Victoria looked up and saw a very tiny hedgehog looking absolutely terrified, and clinging on to a branch for dear life. "How on earth did he get up there in the first place?" asked Victoria.

The hedgehogs answered in a chorus, "That rotten Elf put him up there."

Without waiting to hear any more Victoria flew up into the branches of the tree, picked up the tiny

creature, and brought him safely down to his brothers. Victoria looked at Sugar and said, "I think it's time we had a word with Eric and Ben before they get up to any more mischief," and she flew off towards Ben's house.

On the way there Victoria came across a spider busily weaving webs and muttering to herself. "You look busy," said Victoria.

"Yes," said the spider, "I have to be, that awful Elf came flying through here and ripped down all my beautiful webs. Now I'll have to weave them all again."

Victoria didn't need to ask "which awful Elf" the spider was talking about. She knew it had to be Eric.

When Victoria arrived at Ben's house she found the

two Elves throwing mud pies at each other. "Hello, you two," said Eric, "why don't you join us? This mud is ever so sticky, it makes a lovely mess."

"No thank you," said Victoria primly, "we've come to ask you not to play any more nasty tricks on the woodland creatures. What you did to the mouse, the hedgehogs and the spider was very unkind."

But Eric just laughed. "Oh that," he said. "It was just a bit of fun. Haven't any of you woodland creatures got a sense of humour?" And with that he threw a big mud pie at the two fairies. Victoria ducked out of the way but the lump of black gooey mud landed right in the middle of Sugar's sparkling white dress. It slithered down the front leaving a long, black stain, and then sploshed onto her spotless little shoes. Sugar looked a mess, and was so upset that she burst into tears.

"Silly ninny," said Eric, and he started to laugh at Sugar, and Ben joined in. Victoria was so angry. Obviously it wasn't worth trying to talk to Eric, and Ben was no better. She took Sugar's hand and flew straight home.

During the rest of that week Victoria and Sugar avoided Ben and Eric. But they kept hearing the most terrible stories about them. The squirrels had their nuts stolen and scattered all over the woodland floor. Badgers had found the entrance to their homes blocked up. Birds had been dive-bombed by two noisy, fast flying Elves, and all the young rabbits had been scattered and frightened out of their wits by two Elves pretending to be a pack of dogs. It had taken the adults

hours to find them all, and now everyone was too terrified to come out of their homes.

Everything pointed to Ben and his friend Eric. Victoria was very sad. She and Ben had been friends for a very long time, but Eric was obviously a bad influence on him. And to make matters worse Eric had decided that he was enjoying himself so much, that he would stay longer than two weeks. When everyone in the Great Wood heard that they all groaned. Eric was making life so unpleasant for them that everyone was scared and miserable. The last straw came when the two Elves set fire to old hedgehog's bed.

"It's just a pile of old leaves," laughed Eric. "The old fool will soon find something else." He thought it was a huge joke. But no one in the Great Wood was amused, and Victoria Plum decided that this time they'd gone too far. Eric had to go.

Victoria's Secret Plan

One afternoon all the woodland elders gathered in Victoria's old tree house to try to find a way of making Eric leave the Great Wood and never return. They talked and talked for hours. And eventually Victoria came up with a plan. She told everyone what she had in mind, and they all agreed it was a very good plan and they should get to work the very next day.

In the morning Eric and Ben were walking through the Great Wood, kicking stones along the path as they went. Suddenly they heard two young rabbits whispering behind a hedge. Eric heard one say to the other, "I'm told it's the most wonderful treasure. Something more precious and beautiful than anything we've ever seen in the Great Wood before."

Eric stopped dead. He was a very greedy Elf by nature, and couldn't resist the thought of buried treasure. He hopped over the hedge and pulled the young rabbits' ears. He looked at them menacingly. "Tell me where this treasure is," said Eric, "or I'll tie your ears in knots and you'll never get them out."

The young rabbits started shivering with fear. "I

don't know where the treasure is," said the eldest rabbit. "I just heard one of the squirrels saying that there was buried treasure near the Great Wood and that someone had hidden a treasure map in the old woodpecker's nest in the big oak tree."

Eric's eyes widened. "Fantastic," he said. "Come on, Ben, let's find the map before someone else hears of this treasure," and with that he spitefully pulled the rabbits' tails, and flew off.

When both Eric and Ben had gone, Victoria flew down from the trees where she'd been hiding. The two rabbits looked very pleased with themselves and said, "Did we

do everything right, Victoria?'' And Victoria said, "Yes, rabbits, you were both very brave. Now let's see what happens next.''

Right in the middle of the wood Ben and Eric found the old Oak Tree and saw the hole where the woodpecker had made his nest the year before. Eric squeezed through the tiny hole, and inside found a piece of crumpled paper. It was the map. "I've found it!'' he cried excitedly and without waiting to stop for Ben, flew off through the trees, laughing and shouting.

When Ben caught up with him Eric had already reached the edge of the Great Wood and was looking at the map. It showed the path leading to the garden of the Big House and the low hedge that sheltered the vegetables grown by Mr. P, the gardener. And there, just by the side of hedge, was a large 'X'.

"That's it," said Eric. "That's where the treasure's been buried," and once more, without waiting for Ben, flew off towards the vegetable garden. When they arrived at the spot, Ben was dismayed. "It can't be there," he said, "that's right in the middle of the compost heap."

But Eric was so greedy he really didn't care. He dived

straight into the middle of the smelly heap and started digging. "Come on!" he shouted, and Ben, very reluctantly, joined in.

The compost heap was very slimy and very smelly. It was full of old leaves, dead grass, rotting cabbage and potato peelings. Within minutes the two Elves were covered in a rotting, smelly mess, but they went on digging and burrowing.

At last Eric uncovered a small box. "I've found it!" he

shouted with glee, and threw open the lid. Inside were a pair of beautiful, tiny shoes. Each one was pure white and sugar frosted, with delicate pink bows on the top and tiny silver bells on the toes. They were the most beautiful shoes you could ever wish to see.

Eric was very angry. "That's not treasure!" he roared. "It's just a sissy pair of shoes."

Suddenly Sugar Plum flew down from the trees and hovered above them. "So that's where my best party shoes are," she said. "I wonder how on earth they got there," and light as a feather she plucked them out of the box and flew back to the top of the trees. Within seconds the garden was full of woodland creatures all crowding around the compost heap, giggling and laughing. "What a terrible smell," said one. "Must be some old rubbish Mr. P has thrown away," said another.

Eric was furious and his face turned red with temper. "You tricked me," he said. "There wasn't any treasure at all." Eric looked so silly that no one was frightened of him any more, and one of the squirrels said boldly, "What's the matter, Eric, don't you have a sense of humour?" and everyone burst out laughing again.

Eric roared at them, "I'm not staying here," and then he said to Ben, "and don't ever expect me to come and

visit you again." Then he flew off in a rage, leaving behind a trail of dead leaves and smelly cabbage. Everyone cheered and said, "Good riddance."

Victoria flew down from the trees where she'd been watching and landed next to Ben. All the animals fell silent. Ben had been left sitting on top of the smelly compost heap looking very foolish and feeling very sorry for himself. There was no need to be cross with Ben. Everyone could see that he was sorry for all the horrid things he'd done. So Victoria took Ben's hand and walked with him to the edge of the garden. She was trying to be very stern and look very cross. But she couldn't pretend for long and suddenly began to laugh

helplessly, and then everyone joined in.

"I'm so sorry, Ben," Victoria said. "But you really do look ridiculous! And you smell absolutely disgusting." And with that she threw a handful of fairy dust over him to take away the smell and the slime of the compost heap. When Ben was quite clean, Sugar Plum flew down to join them.

"I'm so glad that horrid Elf has gone," said Sugar. "Because I really do think you're a much nicer person without him."

Victoria and all the woodland creatures agreed. But Ben didn't say a word. He was much too busy trying to pretend that he wasn't blushing!